AUTHOR'S PREFACE TO THE 10th EDITION

Since it was launched in 1985 this collection of tips and techniques has become Management Pocketbook's best seller. I've updated it several times and it has remained a popular, practical patchwork of advice for front line HRD practitioners.

Once again, for the milestone 10th edition, we have decided to revise the content to reflect the developments that have taken place in our roles and in the training function itself. Notably there's a whole new section covering the 'Facilitraining Rainbow' which Paul Donovan and I have developed to help trainers decide which delivery style is most appropriate for their situation.

Although, happily, the role of trainer remains vital in the learning process, the training function is broadening to include a whole range of professionals from Training Needs Analysts to Performance Consultants, Process Monitors and Training Evaluation Specialists. Above all, great progress has been made in our knowledge of how the brain works and, therefore, how people learn and remember training messages.

This new edition attempts to reflect these changes and includes a consistent set of delightfully right-brained graphics from Phil Hailstone.

For the sake of specificity, however, it still concentrates on tools for the **front line training deliverer** - whether he or she is called an Instructor, a Teacher, a Course Leader or, as is more often the case, a **Trainer**.

John Townsend, Ferney

CONTENTS

INTRODUCTION 1
3D trainer grid, the expert

LEARNING THEORY 5
Brain power, retention and recall, VHF messages, donkey bridges, mind set

LEARNING ENVIRONMENT 23
Checklist, seating patterns, setting up the room, media

PREPARING TO TRAIN 35
The 5 W's, structuring, memory techniques, timing, training methods, trainer preparation

TRAINING DELIVERY 47
Names, icebreakers, enthusiasm, the 'Facilitraining Rainbow', presenting/demonstrating, teaching/Socratic direction, facilitating discussion/brainstorming, dealing with difficult questions and 'outbursts', dealing with challengers

AUDIO VISUAL SUPPORT 79
VHF communication, vistips, flip tips, health warning!, slide tips, OHP, whiteboard, video/DVD, talking wall, music, anecdotes, metaphors, parables, touch, taste, smell, Murphy's Law, feedback

GROUP & INDIVIDUAL EXERCISES 109
Icebreakers, quiz, case studies, video recording, role playing, project work, instruments

THE TRAINER'S POCKETBOOK

By John Townsend

Illustrations by Phil Hailstone

"The most creatively practical book on the subject. Even the most experienced trainer will find a handful of ideas."
Management Centre Europe, Brussels

"The Trainer's Pocketbook is an extremely useful collection of helpful hints, suggestions and reminders for trainers and presenters. It is standard handout material for all instructors we train."
Richard Franklin, Education Programme Manager, Hewlett-Packard, France

© John Townsend 1985, 1987, 1988, 1990, 1991, 1993, 1994, 1996, 2002, 2003.

First published in 1985 by Thamesman as The Instructor's Pocketbook. All subsequent editions published by:

Management Pocketbooks Ltd
Laurel House, Station Approach, Alresford, Hants SO24 9JH, U.K.
Tel: +44 (0)1962 735573 Fax: +44 (0)1962 733637
E-mail: sales@pocketbook.co.uk Website: www.pocketbook.co.uk

Second edition	The Instructor's Pocketbook	1987
Third edition	The Instructor's Pocketbook	1988
Fourth edition	The Instructor's Pocketbook	1990
Fifth edition	The Instructor's Pocketbook	1991
Sixth edition	The Instructor's Pocketbook	1993
Seventh edition	The Instructor's Pocketbook	1994
Eighth edition	as The Trainer's Pocketbook	1996
Ninth edition	The Trainer's Pocketbook	2002
Tenth edition	The Trainer's Pocketbook	2003

Reprinted 2004 (revised), 2005, 2006.

ISBN-13   978 1 903776 16 2
ISBN-10   1 903776 16 3

British Library Cataloguing-in-Publication Data – A catalogue record for this book is available from the British Library.

Printed in England.

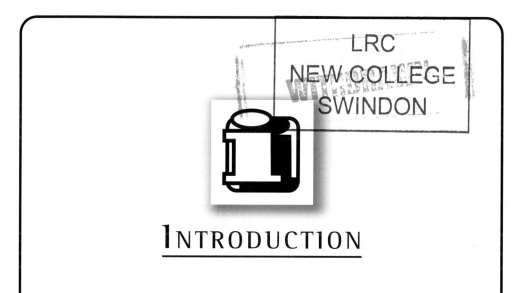

INTRODUCTION

INTRODUCTION

Training is a valued and rewarding profession because it is dedicated to helping people grow. A Master Trainer's performance can be measured on 3 dimensions:

Subject Matter Knowledge and Experience

- Technical competence in subject matter(s) taught ● Practical 'on the job' experience
- Academic qualifications ● Knowledge of the training function
- Competence in promoting training

Trainer Techniques and Skills (Design and delivery of Training Courses)

- Training needs analysis ● Applying learning theory to course design ● Keeping trainee recall high ● Making learning fun ● Performing (voice control, eye contact, body language, etc) ● Developing and using audio-visual support
- Leading discussions ● Creating and conducting exercises ● Training evaluation

Concern and Availability to Facilitate Learning

- Empathy ● Listening skills ● Asking and answering questions ● Dealing with 'difficult' trainees ● Facilitating ● Adapting style/content to fit trainees' needs

3D TRAINER GRID

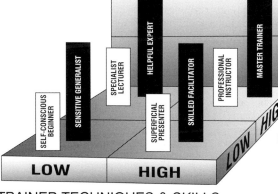

CONCERN & AVAILABILITY
(To Facilitate Learning)

HIGH

LOW

SELF-CONSCIOUS BEGINNER

SENSITIVE GENERALIST

SPECIALIST LECTURER

HELPFUL EXPERT

SUPERFICIAL PRESENTER

SKILLED FACILITATOR

PROFESSIONAL INSTRUCTOR

MASTER TRAINER

LOW | HIGH

SUBJECT MATTER KNOWLEDGE & EXPERIENCE

LOW | HIGH

TRAINER TECHNIQUES & SKILLS
(Design & Delivery of Training Courses)

(3)

Beware of the Expert!

A 'Has-Been'

A 'Drip under pressure'

LEARNING THEORY

LEARNING THEORY

BRAINS
HOW ADULTS LEARN

- If they want and need to
- By linking learning to past, present or future experience
- By practising what they have been taught
- With help and guidance
- In an informal and non-threatening environment

BRAINS

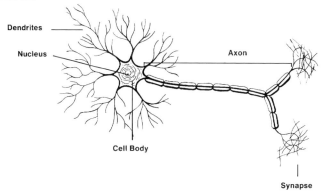

Neurologists are now saying that the average brain contains
100 billion brain cells (neurons). Each one is like a tiny tree with messages passing from
branches to roots, each making hundreds of connections to other cells as we think. The
total 'megabyte' capacity is inconceivably large.

LEARNING THEORY

BRAINS
DO BRAINS DECLINE?

The myth that brain power declines with age has finally been exploded.

- If the brain is stimulated **no matter at what age** new 'twigs' will grow on each brain cell's branches and increase the total number of possible connections

- Some of the world's most creative people have been exceptionally prolific at advanced ages (Gauguin, Michelangelo, Haydn, Picasso)

- We generate new brain connections more rapidly than the average loss of brain cells - even if we lose 10,000 brain cells a day from birth, the total number lost at age 80 would be less than 3%

LEARNING THEORY

BRAINS

SPEED/PREFERENCES

Neurologists have a lot to teach teachers and trainers! Recent experiments in Brussels have shown that:

- The average person can think at 800 words per minute but the average trainer can only talk at 120 wpm - **so we must give our participants something interesting to do with their spare 680 wpm!**

- The brain goes into 'auto shut-off' after only 10 minutes if it is not given something to stimulate it - **so we must vary the media and give multi-channel messages!**

- When a message is given once, the brain remembers 10% one year later; when it is given six times, recall rises to 90% - **so we must repeat, recap and review**

- The brain prefers: rounded diagrams and figures to square ones; Times and Helvetica typefaces; dark letters on light background; colour, colour, colour!!!

BRAINS

RETENTION: THE PROOF

It may be that our brains retain every piece of information they ever receive:

- **Death-type experiences:** people snatched from death say that their entire life flashed before them

- **Hypnosis:** under competent supervision hypnotees have unlocked vast memory banks

- **Surprise stimulation:** the 'déja vu' experience may be triggered by sights, sounds or smells

- **Experiments:** in experiments where patients received electrode treatment, they 're-lived' past, forgotten experiences

- **Mnemonics:** using special 'memory systems' normal people can rival famous stage magicians

BRAINS

RECALL: 5 MAIN FACTORS

FIRST — We are more likely to remember the beginning of events or the first in a series of events

REVIEWED — Recall falls rapidly after 24 hours without review

OUTSTANDING — We remember unusual things exceedingly well!

LINKED — Recall is high for things which are linked by mnemonics or analogy

LAST — We are more likely to remember the end of events or the last in a series of events

The Finnish **FROLL**
(A cousin of the Norwegian Troll)

(11)

BRAINS
RECALL OVER TIME

BRAINS
HOW TO KEEP RECALL HIGH

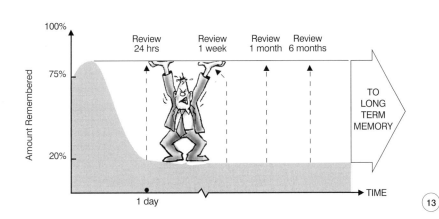

BRAINS

BRAINS - LEFT AND RIGHT

Logical

- Speech
- Calculations
- Intellectual Analysis
- Reading
- Writing
- Naming
- Ordering
- Sequencing
- Complex motor sequences
- Critique
- Evaluation
- Logic

c**R**eative

- Creativity (new combinations)
- Artistic activity
- Musical ability/Rhythm
- Emotions
- Recognition
- Comprehension
- Perception of abstract patterns
- Spatial abilities
- Facial expressions
- Holistic ability
- Intuition
- Images
- Colour

BRAINS

STIMULATING THE LEFT AND RIGHT BRAIN

Professional trainers encourage learners to use both sides of the brain. Experiments have shown that:

- People who have been trained to use one side of the brain more than the other (accountants, engineers, versus artists, musicians) find it difficult to 'switch' when necessary

- When the weaker side is stimulated and encouraged to co-operate with the stronger side there is a greater synergy (1 + 1 = 5!)

Example: Newton understood the theory of gravity while day-dreaming

Applications: Trainers should combine analytical exercises with creative, expressive activities

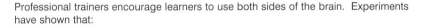

15

BRAINS

VHF

To help trainees use both sides of the brain we must remember that information is stored with **V**ery **H**igh **F**requency - in VHF!

VISUAL
- Pictures • Scenes • Images • Logos • Diagrams • Graphs
- Charts • Photos • Drawings

HEARING
- Words • Music • Sounds • Accents
- Conversations

FEELING
- Emotions • Smells • Tastes
- Tactile experiments • Pain/Comfort

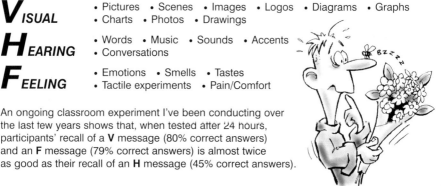

An ongoing classroom experiment I've been conducting over the last few years shows that, when tested after 24 hours, participants' recall of a **V** message (80% correct answers) and an **F** message (79% correct answers) is almost twice as good as their recall of an **H** message (45% correct answers).

BRAINS

MULTI-CHANNEL MESSAGES

Because people can store information in the left **and** the right brain in the form of pictures (**V**), words (**H**) or sensations and feelings (**F**) we, as professional trainers, must give **multi-channel messages.**

This means giving colourful visual back up to our verbal messages at the same time as appealing to trainees' emotions and senses.

These messages will be stored simultaneously in several parts of the left and right brain and therefore multiply the chances of recall.

BRAINS

MNEMONICS

Many devices exist to help people recall multi-channel messages. The Germans call them 'donkey bridges' (Eselsbrücke) because they help the donkey of ignorance across the bridge to knowledge! They are **mnemonics** (memory devices) which **link together** two or more pieces of information. By linking together visual, hearing and/or feeling data, the donkey bridge creates a distinct and more memorable whole.
Example: the FROLL on page 11!

Note: A mnemonic (not newmonic!) is from a Greek word and means **any** kind of memory device, not just first letter acronyms.

Interestingly, neurologists report that donkey bridges actually do provide a link across the brain's **real** bridge between the right and left brain (the corpus collosum)!

BRAINS

DONKEY BRIDGES

Here are 5 kinds of donkey bridges which trainers can use to revolutionise trainee recall!

- **First Letter Acronym** (Flac!)
  Take the first letter of every word or phrase to be remembered and create a new word and (if possible) image
  Example: As a trainer you should **pamper** the audience with your voice by using pampers - **P**rojection **A**rticulation **M**odulation **P**ronunciation **E**nunciation **R**epetition **S**peed (see page 57)

- **First Letter Phrase** (Flep!)
  Create a phrase where each word begins with the letter of each thing to be remembered in a list
  Example: **R**ichard **O**f **Y**ork **G**ave **B**attle **I**n **V**ain
  to remember the colour sequence of **R**ed **O**range **Y**ellow **G**reen **B**lue **I**ndigo and **V**iolet in a rainbow

BRAINS

DONKEY BRIDGES

- **Sounds**
  Select music, songs or sound effects which will remind your
  trainees of your messages when they hear them in the future
  Examples: Use a 'polka' (POLCA) as the theme tune for a management
  course on **P**lanning **O**rganising **L**eading **C**ontrolling **A**chieving;
  Tina Turner's 'You're The Best' for a sales team course

- **Rhymes & Slogans**
  Create a memorable rhyme or slogan to 'anchor' your training message
  Examples: For a trainer it's 'Optional to be a professional'; Peace Corps
  water-saving slogan for the Caribbean: 'When it's yellow let it
  mellow, when it's brown, flush it down!'

- **Logos and Image Association** (Lima!)
  Design a logo for your course; create visual aids which help
  trainees remember key messages by associating them with
  a powerful picture - logos last longer!
  Example: Think of any flag or any company logo and reflect on
  all the messages this simple shape brings to your mind

(20)

MIND SET

However hard we try to keep trainee recall high, the enemy is **Mind Set**. When people hear or see something that clashes with their beliefs or values, they experience **Cognitive Dissonance**. Because of the discomfort caused by this dissonance, they will either justify their present beliefs/behaviour or distort the new information so that it no longer challenges their 'world view'. Some famous people have been victims of their mind set!

- 'Who the hell wants to hear actors talk?' (Harry Warner, 1927)

- 'There is no likelihood that man can ever tap the power of the atom'
  (Robert Millikan, Nobel Prize, 1923)

- 'Sensible and responsible women do not want to vote'
  (Grover Cleveland, 1927)

- 'Heavier-than-air flying machines are impossible'
  (Lord Kelvin, 1895)

MIND SET

Faced with inevitable and totally natural problems of mind set, we trainers must help our trainees to overcome the discomfort caused by cognitive dissonance. Like Shakespeare's Mark Antony, we must start from **their** point of view ('Brutus was an honourable man') and find a **WIFT** (**W**hat's **I**n it **F**or **T**hem?) to help them change their minds.

By concentrating on WIFTs we help them to justify changing their skills, knowledge or attitudes by providing a real need to do so.

Example: Faced with a salesperson whose mind set is 'I should be out selling, not listening to this nonsense', you should concentrate on how your course can help her sell more.

Exercises:

- Think of one of your own courses. What WIFTs can you think of for a 'dinosaur' trainee whose mind set is 'our present system has worked very well up to now'?

- How could you find WIFTs to overcome the following mind set:
  'What can this upstart teach **me**; s/he's half my age!'?

LEARNING ENVIRONMENT

THE IDEAL ENVIRONMENT
CHECKLIST

- Good audio visual equipment (see appropriate section)

- Appropriate seating patterns (pp 25-30)

- Comfortable chairs

- Good writing surface for each participant

- Thermostatically controlled temperature (ideal ambient temperature = 18° C)

- Independently controlled ventilation (air conditioning or windows)

- Good supply of coffee/light lunches

- Adequately sound-proofed room, with 5 square metres space per participant

- Natural daylight (windows with blinds/curtains), with minimum 500 lux lighting

- Central electrical commands (lights, audio visual, etc)

LEARNING ENVIRONMENT

SEATING PATTERNS

1. 'U' shape

Advantages
- Businesslike
- Trainer can walk into 'U'
- Generally good participant visibility
- Standard, therefore non-threatening

Disadvantages
- Somewhat formal; needs ice-breaking
- Some participants masked by audio visual equipment
- Front participants constantly at 60-90° (neck ache)
- Rear participants are far from screen/flip chart

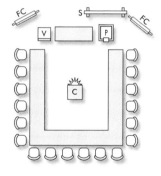

FC = Flip Chart / P = Projector / S = Screen / C = Carousel / V = Video

SEATING PATTERNS

2. 'V' shape

Advantages
- Best pattern for visibility/neck ache
- Optimum trainer/participant contact
- Less formal and intimidating than 'U'

Disadvantages
- Space requirements (only small groups)

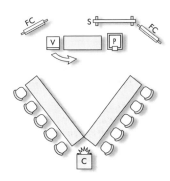

FC = Flip Chart / P = Projector / S = Screen / C = Carousel / V = Video

SEATING PATTERNS

3. Herring Bone

Advantages
- Space effective for large numbers
- All participants at good angle to screen/flip chart, etc
- Trainer can walk down 'spine'

Disadvantages
- Several participants 'masked' by others
- Reminiscent of school
- Encourages dysfunctional groupings
- Rear participants far from screen/flip chart, etc
- Relatively poor participant/trainer contact

FC = Flip Chart / P = Projector / S = Screen / C = Carousel / V = Video

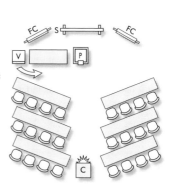

SEATING PATTERNS

4. 'Bistro'

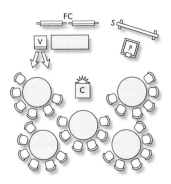

Advantages

- Ideal for 'teambuilding' sessions and small group workshops
- Informal: encourages maximum trainee participation/identification
- Original: encourages open-mindedness
- Trainer can 'circulate'

Disadvantages

- Some participants have poor visibility or may be constantly at an angle to screen/flip chart
- May foster lack of attention and encourage side conversations
- Encourages splinter group identification

FC = Flip Chart / P = Projector / S = Screen / C = Carousel / V = Video

SEATING PATTERNS

5. Circle

Advantages

- Ideal for sensitivity training sessions
- Encourages maximum participant involvement
- Excellent trainer/participant contact
- Minimum side conversations;
  no informal group formation

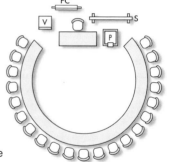

Disadvantages

- Difficult to find tables which can be set up in a circle
- Some participants have poor visibility/neck ache
- Without suitable tables participants may feel unnecessarily 'exposed'
- Overtones of 'touchy/feely' style encounter groups

FC = Flip Chart / P = Projector / S = Screen / C = Carousel / V = Video

SEATING PATTERNS

6. Amphitheatre

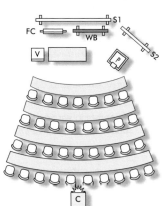

Advantages
- If room is well designed, excellent visibility and acoustics
- Very space-effective
- Good for lecture-type presentations

Disadvantages
- Very poor trainer/participant contact
- Difficult to set up unless room is designed with permanent seating
- Back rows must be elevated
- Very university-like

FC = Flip Chart / P = Projector / S = Screen / C = Carousel /
V = Video / WB = Whiteboard

LEARNING ENVIRONMENT

SEATING PATTERNS

PSYCHOLOGY

- Research shows that distance reduces participation - trainees in back rows are less likely to participate than those in front

- Any kind of 'row' reduces interaction: it is difficult for those in the back row to hear front row contributions and for those in the front row to twist round to interact with people behind

- Changes in seating patterns from one session to another can be psychologically upsetting for participants

- At repetitive sessions participants will invariably sit in the same place

- Angry or cynical participants will attempt to move away from a group seating pattern

SETTING UP THE ROOM

MEDIA

VARYING THE MEDIA

As a general rule the learning environment should provide a change of pace/medium/subject/blood circulatory pattern every 10 minutes to avoid 'auto shut-off' (see page 9).

The professional trainer will, therefore, plan seminar coverage so that new audio-visual interventions, and new topics, come at fairly regular 10 minute intervals.

S/he will also plan for regular discussion periods, small group work or 'stretch breaks' to fight the descending learning curve.

Lastly, voice control (pitch, volume, modulation) can help change the pace of a seminar.

PREPARING TO TRAIN

PREPARING TO TRAIN

THE 5 W'S
QUESTIONS TO ASK

The success of a seminar, course or instructional module depends on a great number of variables. Before preparing yourself to train, you must answer 5 questions specifically - the 5 **W**'s!

WHY?
- Ask why you are training at all. What are the trainees' objectives? What should trainees think or do at the end of the course?

WHAT?
- Ask what you can put over in the available time. At what intellectual level will you pitch your teaching? What audio visual aids will you need?

WHO?
- Analyse the trainee group: Age? Nationality? Level? Language abilities? Prior experience? Expectations? Mind set?

WHEN?
- Ask whether the timing of the course is good for you and for them. Period of year? Weekdays/weekends? Morning? Afternoon? Evening?

WHERE?
- Ask about and prepare for environment. Building? Room? Layout? Seating patterns? Interruptions? Temperature? Noise?

STRUCTURE

HOW TO DESIGN A LEARNING EXPERIENCE

B. GUNAR EDEG R.A.F. (B) *
The Icelandic pilot who joined the Royal Air Force
('B' Squadron)

* This mnemonic device will help you remember the
14 vital steps in designing a well-structured and
memorable learning experience.

PREPARING TO TRAIN

STRUCTURE

DESIGN: STEP 1

BANG
- Always start with a learning 'hook' or attention-getter

GAP
- Establish the gap between participants' present skills/knowledge and those to be acquired during the course

UNDERSTAND
- Check that participants understand the existence and size of skills/knowledge gap

NEED
- Establish the need for participants to close the skills/knowledge gap

ASK/ANSWER
- Ask and answer questions to check participants' individual needs (encourage those with smaller gap/need to help with 'teaching')

ROUTE MAP
- Outline course coverage, stressing results to be achieved (during and after the course) in closing skills/knowledge gap

STRUCTURE
DESIGN: STEP 2

Explain

Demonstrate

Exercise

Guide/correct

- Explain each new skill/learning in digestible chunks using appropriate **V**isual, **H**earing and **F**eeling support (see page 80)

- Demonstrate skills and/or show how knowledge applies to them; use **VHF** support

- Allow participants to exercise each new skill or to feedback their understanding of new knowledge

- Show participants how well they have learned and correct any inadequacies

STRUCTURE

DESIGN: STEP 3

$\boldsymbol{R}_{ECAP}$

- Review all learning points at end of each module (or beginning of next); use **VHF** support

$\boldsymbol{A}_{CTION\ PLAN}$

- Agree on an action plan for the transfer of new skills or knowledge to real life

$\boldsymbol{F}_{OLLOW-UP}$

- Agree on any follow-up or refresher

$\boldsymbol{B}_{ANG}$

- Always finish with a succinct and provocative encapsulation of the learning experience

MEMORY TECHNIQUES

NAME CARDS

Unless you are in a formal school setting, make sure that each participant is provided with a ready-made or do-it-yourself 'tent card' for his/her name. Ask for big bold letters so you can read the name from any part of the teaching area.

Tip   With cardboard tent cards,
       bend over a corner to keep
       the card from collapsing.

COURSE TIMING

DOWN TIME

In a training day of 9 hours (08.30 - 17.30) always plan for down time as follows:

- Latecomers, settling, housekeeping = 10 mins

- Coffee/Tea breaks = 20 + 20 = 40 mins
  (even if you have planned 15 minute breaks!)

- Lunch and 're-settling' after lunch = 75 mins
  (even if you have planned 1 hour!)

- Stretch breaks, breaking into syndicates
  and other miscellaneous
  down time = 25 mins

  Total = 2 hrs 30 mins

COURSE TIMING

TIMING TIPS

- Always keep a clock or watch on your desk - but don't rely on looking at the watch on your wrist

- Use a chronometer or good kitchen timer for timing break-out sessions, separate modules, etc

- Always allow time for discussion - build it in to your course plan

TRAINING METHODS

EFFECTIVENESS OF DIFFERENT METHODS

Ranking of methods depending on TEACHING GOALS (1 = high, 8 = low)

METHOD	KNOWLEDGE ACQUISITION	ATTITUDE CHANGE	PROBLEM-SOLVING SKILLS	INTER-PERSONAL SKILLS	PARTICIPANT ACCEPTANCE	KNOWLEDGE RETENTION
CASE STUDY	4	5	1	5	1	4
WORKSHOP	1	3	4	4	5	2
LECTURE	8	7	7	8	7	3
GAMES	5	4	2	3	2	7
FILMS	6	6	8	6	4	5
PROGRAMMED INSTR.	3	8	6	7	8	1
ROLE-PLAYING	2	2	3	1	3	6
'T' GROUP	7	1	5	2	6	8

Source J. Newstrom "Evaluating Effectiveness of Training Methods

TRAINER PREPARATION

HOW TO BEAT MURPHY!

- Always carry a checklist of material, equipment, etc, to the training site

- Arrive at the training site at least one hour before the start of the programme to prepare material and equipment

- Take at least 15 minutes from this time to prepare yourself:
  - physically; centring energy, grooming, posture and breathing
  - mentally; visualising the participant group, trying to imagine how they are feeling and asking/answering the question, 'How can I best **help** these people to change and grow, given the programme objectives and organisational culture?'

PREPARING TO TRAIN

TRAINER PREPARATION

PERSONAL STANDARDS

- Consciously manage personal energy levels by avoiding temptations to over-eat, over-drink or under-sleep before or during the programme

- Keep physically fit with at least one type of exercise per week

TRAINING DELIVERY

GENERAL

NAMES AND FACES

When faced with a room full of new trainees you will need to remember their names

- Listen to name
- Spell it in your head
- Repeat name as often as possible during training event
- Look for an outstanding facial feature
- Exaggerate the feature
- Associate
  Mrs Hawkes   =   beaked nose
  Mr White   =   sickness/fear/clown
  Mr Metropoulos =   big town, city slicker

This will ensure you can address
(and impress) them during coffee
break, lunch, etc.

ICEBREAKERS

Professional trainers always start with an **Icebreaker** or **Inclusion Activity** (see page 110 for some examples).

WHY?

- When trainees arrive in a training room they are usually a loose mix of individuals with different mind sets

- At the beginning of a course, trainees are usually **not** thinking about the trainer or the course content but about their neighbour, coffee time for phoning/messages, the end of the day for errands, sights, sounds and smells in the room, etc

- An inclusion activity will make them feel **included** and, if well designed, help them to relate to the others in the group; it can also provide a bridge into the course itself

- Above all it puts the spotlight on **them** (the most important people in the room) and takes it off **you** and allows you to relax into the course

ICEBREAKERS

WHAT? A good inclusion activity should be:

Foolproof: has been tested and works!

Amusing: trainees should enjoy it

Bridged: linked to the course subject (if possible)

Unique: trainees should not have done it before

Lively: has movement, exchange and chatter

Optimistic: is positive and non-threatening

Uncomplicated: is easy to explain and organise

Short: lasts between 5 and 10 minutes

This donkey bridge was developed by
Richard Hamilton and the 'Red Team' at
a WWF Train the Trainer Course.

ENTHUSIASM

YOU GOTTA BELIEVE!

- If you're not enthusiastic about your subject, how can you expect the trainees to be!!

- Consciously use your eyes and eyebrows to communicate enthusiasm

- Always keep a sparkle in your voice

- Fight boredom of repetitive sessions by introducing new anecdotes, examples, etc, or by changing lesson structure

The Facilitraining Rainbow

HIGH

AMOUNT OF INTERACTION WITH PARTICIPANTS

SOCRATIC DIRECTION

FACILITATING DISCUSSION

How to decide which Facilitraining style/strategy to use

TEACHING

BRAINSTORMING

DEMONSTRATING

PROCESS MONITORING

PRESENTING

Plenty		Very Little
	TIME AVAILABLE	
High		Low
	PARTICIPANTS' PRESENT LEVEL OF KNOWLEDGE	
High (Attitude Change)		(Knowledge Acquisition) Low
	OWNERSHIP OF OUTCOME NEEDED	
Many Options		Only One Option
	CERTAINTY OF 'ONE BEST WAY'	
To discuss	To be consulted	To be told
	CULTURAL EXPECTATIONS	
High		Low
	YOUR SKILL AS A FACILITATOR	

LOW

HIGH

← FACILITATOR'S CONTRIBUTION TO CONTENT →

colour version on inside of cover

THE FACILITRAINING RAINBOW (1)

The Facilitraining Rainbow is a simple model to help trainers decide which style of training best suits which situation. The various criteria in the middle of the rainbow will help you determine whether to be more to the right of the rainbow (presenting mode) or more to the left (facilitating mode). Each of the seven styles combines varying amounts of interaction with participants with the trainer's own input on content and blend into each other as you 'surf' the rainbow.

PRESENTING (low interaction/high contribution)

The classic and often necessary style to put across information. However, as competition from the multimedia environment grows, trainers need to perform at an increasingly professional pitch so as not to be zapped by participants.

DEMONSTRATING (medium to low interaction/high contribution)

Not as 'one way' as presenting, demonstrating involves interaction with participants in as much as they are asked to try out in some way what has been presented.

THE FACILITRAINING RAINBOW (2)

TEACHING (medium to high interaction/medium to high contribution)

When in the classic teaching mode, the trainer provides structured learning experiences and guides participants towards pre-determined learning objectives. He or she nevertheless provides some latitude for interpretation at an individual level.

SOCRATIC DIRECTION (high interaction/low to high contribution)

This is the 'maieutic' method pioneered by Socrates whereby the facilitrainer asks questions and then reformulates the answers as necessary to lead participants to a desired learning outcome. The rainbow provides for a wide range of 'leading' strategies from relatively open to relatively closed. The common element in all Socratic styles is the amount of interaction. It is based on the premise that 'people don't argue with their own data' even when it is massaged and channelled towards a hidden learning outcome – as long as the 'facipulation' is done professionally and sincerely.

THE FACILITRAINING RAINBOW (3)

FACILITATING DISCUSSION (medium to high interaction/low to medium contribution)

When using this style the facilitator interacts quite often with participants to invite opinions, control the process and give own opinions (if only to provoke more discussion).

BRAINSTORMING (low to medium interaction/low contribution)

Here the facilitator conducts a classic brainstorming session – interacting with participants only to encourage them to give their ideas but hardly ever evaluating or adding ideas.

PROCESS MONITORING (low interaction/low contribution)

As the 'guardian of the process' the facilitator makes no personal contribution to the content of the discussion but occasionally regulates the flow of participants' contributions according to a previously agreed set of process rules.

PRESENTING / DEMONSTRATING

NERVES: THE MURPHY MONKEY

As you get up to speak, it's as if a monkey has suddenly jumped onto your shoulders. He claws your neck and weighs you down - making your knees feel weak and shaky. As you start to speak, he pulls at your vocal chords and dries up your saliva. He pushes your eyes to the floor, makes your arms feel 10 metres long and attaches a piece of elastic to your belt - pulling you back to the table or wall behind you!

Experienced speakers know about the Murphy monkey. Within the first 30 seconds they throw him to the audience! When you throw the monkey to one of the participants, suddenly the spotlight is on them and not on you. How ...?

- A question, a show of hands, a short 'icebreaker' (participant introductions, an exercise or quiz, etc) a discussion, a 'volunteer' or simply a reference to one or more of the participants - all these are ways of putting the monkey on **their** backs for a few moments

  This takes the pressure off you and gives you time to relax, smile and get ready to communicate your message loud and clear.

PRESENTING / DEMONSTRATING

USING YOUR VOICE

PROJECTION — Speak louder than usual; throw your voice to back of room

ARTICULATION — Don't swallow words
Beware of verbal 'tics'

MODULATION — Vary tone and pitch; be dramatic, confidential and/or triumphant

PRONUNCIATION — Watch tonic accents; check difficult words; beware of malapropisms

ENUNCIATION — Over emphasise
Accentuate syllables

REPETITION — Repeat key phrases with different vocal emphasis

SPEED — Use delivery speed to manipulate the audience; **fast** delivery to excite and stimulate; **slow** delivery to emphasise, awe, dramatise and control

PRESENTING/DEMONSTRATING

YOU CAN'T NOT COMMUNICATE

Research has shown that when someone gives a spoken message the listener's understanding and judgement of that message come from:

7% WORDS

- Words are only labels and listeners put their own interpretation on speakers' words

38% PARALINGUISTICS

- The **way** in which something is said (ie: accent, tone, inflection, etc) is very important to a listener's understanding

55% FACIAL EXPRESSIONS

- What a speaker looks like while delivering a message affects the listener's understanding most

- Research source - Albert Mehrabian

PRESENTING / DEMONSTRATING

LIGHTHOUSE TECHNIQUE

Sweep the audience with your eyes,
staying only 2-3 seconds on
each person - unless in dialogue.

This will give each participant the impression
that you are speaking to him/her personally
and ensure attention, in the same way as
the lighthouse keeps you awake by its
regular sweeping flash of light.
Above all, avoid looking at one
(friendly-looking) member of the
audience or at a fixed (non-threatening)
point on the wall or floor.

PRESENTING / DEMONSTRATING

TYPES OF BODY LANGUAGE

POSTURES & GESTURES
- How do you use hand gestures? Sitting position? Stance?

EYE CONTACT
- How's your 'Lighthouse'?

ORIENTATION
- How do you position yourself in class?

PROXIMITY
- How close do you sit/stand to participants?

LOOKS/APPEARANCE
- Are looks/appearance/dress important?

EXPRESSIONS OF EMOTION
- Are you using facial expressions to express emotion?

PRESENTING / DEMONSTRATING

BODY LANGUAGE TIPS

- Don't be tempted by manual props (pens, pointers, spectacles, etc)

- Don't keep loose change in your pocket

- Be aware of your verbal tics and work on eliminating them (ie: 'OK!' - 'You know' - 'and so forth' - 'Now ...')

- Watch out for furniture!

- Avoid 'closed' or tense body positions

- Don't worry about pacing, leaning, etc

- Check your hair/tie/trousers/dress before standing up!

PRESENTING / DEMONSTRATING

BODY LANGUAGE: HANDS

STEEPLING

- Self Confidence (Intellectual Arrogance)

HAND CLASP

- Anxious, controlled

NOSE TOUCH

- Doubt

'L' CHIN REST

- Critical evaluation

MOUTH BLOCK

- Resisting speech

PRESENTING / DEMONSTRATING

BODY LANGUAGE: STANDING

THUMBS OUT

- In charge! Dominant

FIG LEAF

- Self-control, tense

ARMS OUT

- Open, sincere, conciliatory

TABLE LEAN

- Authoritative, involved

LEAN ON

- Unthreatened, casual belongingness

TEACHING/SOCRATIC DIRECTION

Take a tip from the Ancient Greeks.

If you wish to encourage audience participation to prove a point use **Socratic Direction.**

K now the answers you want

O pen questioning technique

P araphrase participants' answers

S ummarise contributions (flip chart?)

A dd your own points

TEACHING/SOCRATIC DIRECTION

QUESTIONING SKILLS

Closed Questions
- 'Who can tell me on which date?'
- 'Which/what specifically?'

Open Questions
- 'About'   -   'How do you feel about ...?'
- Reflective   -   'You don't feel comfortable with ...?'
- Hypothetical   -   'What do you think would happen if ...?'
- Framing   -   'Help me to see how this fits with ...?'
- Silence   -   ....?
- Statements   -   'Rosemary, you look as if you wanted to say something'

Always avoid: Multiple   -   a string of questions

Leading   -   'Don't you think it would be better to ...?'

TEACHING/SOCRATIC DIRECTION

LUBRICATORS

Verbal
- 'I see'
- 'Ah, ah'
- 'That's interesting!'
- 'Really?'
- 'Go on!'
- 'Tell me more about that'

Non-Verbal
- Nodding
- Constant eye contact
- Leaning forward
- Stepping aside
- Raising eyebrows
- Frowning (encourages clarification)

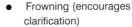

FACILITATING DISCUSSION/BRAINSTORMING

'B'ING

Here are 4 ways to keep a group discussion going:

- **BUILDING**   Build on incomplete answers by adding own comments and asking for agreement or disagreement

- **BOOSTING**   Support timid participants' contributions, boost their confidence and ask for extra comment

- **BLOCKING**   Interrupt dominant/talkative/aggressive participants by asking what others think

- **BANTERING**   Establish non-threatening atmosphere by engaging in friendly repartee with outgoing participants

FACILITATING DISCUSSION/BRAINSTORMING

BRAINSTORMING

A technique for obtaining ideas from a group. Here's how:

_A__SK_ Ask for/provoke ideas; if necessary wait 45 seconds before giving own

_R__ECORD_ Write **all** ideas on a flip chart (number them for future reference) - don't evaluate 'til end

_T__RIGGER_ Use 'B'ing discussion techniques to encourage participants to trigger ideas

_S__UMMARISE_ Summarise and/or regroup ideas; help group to choose best

PROCESS MONITORING

Just about every time you run an exercise you are 'process monitoring'. There is low interaction with participants (they are working more or less on their own) and low contribution from you as to content and outcome (the essence of learning by doing).

The facilitrainers' attitudes and beliefs play an important part in being a good process monitor. Do you really believe that people learn by practising? Can you show them respect by leaving them to discover how to do something on their own, while monitoring only that they are sticking to the structure of the exercises and resisting the temptation to give them the answers too soon?

DEALING WITH DIFFICULT QUESTIONS
REFLECT/DEFLECT

Most participant questions are not questions. They are requests for the spotlight.
If it's one of those rare, closed **real** questions - answer it succinctly. If not, first:

- **REFLECT** back to the questioner what you thought was the question
  ('If I understand correctly, you're asking ...')

Depending on how the questioner 'reformulates' the question, answer it, **OR**

- **DEFLECT** it as follows:
  - **Group** : 'How do the rest of the group feel?'
    : 'Has anyone else had a similar problem?'
  - **Ricochet** : (to one participant) 'Bill, you're an expert on this?'
  - **Reverse** : (back to questioner) 'You've obviously done some thinking on this. What's **your** view?'

DEALING WITH "OUTBURSTS"

ACTIVE LISTENING

Whenever a participant interrupts or responds emotionally during a course s/he is probably overstating his or her feelings in order to justify the 'outburst'. In **every** such case use Active Listening. Never attempt to counter, argue, defend or take sides.

1. Take the outburst as a positive contribution (smile, encourage, nod, use lubricators)
2. Successively reflect back to the participant (in the form of questions) what feelings you heard being expressed. 'You're upset with ...?' 'You're unhappy about ...?' 'You feel that we should ...?' Active listening has 3 advantages:

   ● You show the participant you're interested and not defensive
   ● You allow the participant to confirm that what you heard was what s/he meant **or** to correct your interpretation
   ● You quickly lead the participant to specify the **exact** problem and to suggest a solution

DEALING WITH CHALLENGERS

1. The Heckler

- Probably insecure
- Gets satisfaction from needling
- Aggressive and argumentative

What to do:

- Never get upset
- Find merit, express agreement, move on
- Wait for a mis-statement of fact and then throw it out to the group for correction

DEALING WITH CHALLENGERS

2. The Talker/Know All

- An 'eager beaver'/chatterbox
- A show-off
- Well-informed and anxious to show it

What to do:

- Wait 'til he/she takes a breath, thank, refocus and move on
- Slow him/her down with a tough question
- Jump in and ask for group to comment

DEALING WITH CHALLENGERS

3. The Griper

- Feels 'hard done by'
- Probably has a pet 'peeve'
- Will use you as scapegoat

What to do:

- Get him/her to be specific
- Show that the purpose of your presentation is to be positive and constructive
- Use peer pressure

DEALING WITH CHALLENGERS

4. **The Whisperers** (There's only one; the other is the 'whisperee'!)

- Don't understand what's going on - clarifying or translating
- Sharing anecdotes triggered by your presentation
- Bored, mischievous or hypercritical (unusual)

What to do:

- Stop talking, wait for them to look up and 'non-verbally' ask for their permission to continue
- Use 'lighthouse' technique

75

DEALING WITH CHALLENGERS

5. The Silent One

- Timid, insecure, shy
- Bored, indifferent

What to do:

- Timid?   Ask easy questions; boost his/her ego in discussing answer; refer to by name when giving examples; bolster confidence

- Bored?   Ask tough questions; refer to by name as someone who 'surely knows that ...'; use as helper in exercises

DEALING WITH CHALLENGERS

PSYCHOLOGICAL JUDO
(when classical methods have not worked!)

In physical judo you use the energy of your opponent to cause his downfall by changing your 'push' into 'pull'. In psychological judo you ask the difficult participants to be **even more** difficult. This gives them even more of the spotlight and attention than they wanted and they will use their energy to 'pull back' to avoid ridicule or overkill.

Classical Confrontation   Psychological Judo

* See page 78 for examples

(77)

DEALING WITH CHALLENGERS
PSYCHOLOGICAL JUDO

Examples:

1 The Heckler   Appoint as class 'devil's advocate'. Insist that s/he criticises **whenever** s/he feels you are leading class astray. Demand negative remarks.

2 The Know-All   Agree with and amplify 'know-all' contributions. Ask for expert judgement when none is forthcoming. Get him/her up front to teach short module. Refer constantly to their expertise in subject matter taught.

3 The Griper   Ask for written list of gripes to help class maintain sense of realism. Get him/her to read list at end of day. Add to list whenever possible!

4 The Whisperers State that time is short and ask those who don't understand not to interrupt but to ask their neighbour!

5 The Silent One State that some people are shy and dare not participate. This does not mean they have not understood. Encourage shy ones not to participate.

AUDIO VISUAL SUPPORT
How to use Visual, Hearing and Feeling support

VHF COMMUNICATION

The human brain stores information in VHF – as Visual, Hearing or Feeling data.

Each participant has a preferred channel for remembering data. In my on-going classroom experiment on recall, 51% of participants say that their memory favours visual information, while only 7% prefer words/lectures and sounds. An astonishing 42% say they remember feelings, tastes, smells and tactile experiences best.

In order to 'tune in' to the maximum number of participants' wavelengths, professional speakers use a wide range of transmitters!

V • Imaging • Flip chart • Pinboard • Whiteboard • OHP • Slide projector
• PowerPoint slides • Props and accessories • Video/DVD clips • Word pictures

H • Music (instant access CD's or Minidisks for changes of mood/illustrations)
• Sound effects • Audio gimmicks • Onomatopoeia

F • Music (emotion/mood setting) • Handouts • Verbal descriptions
• Anecdotes • Metaphors • Parables • Smells • Tastes • Cross-sensing

Feelings stay longer than facts!

FIRST AID KIT

TOOLKIT

MASKING TAPE
(for sticking UP flips/
posters and sticking
DOWN dangerous wires)

BEEP

TIMER

THICK COLOURED MARKERS

PENKNIFE

SPARE ACETATES AND OVERHEAD PENS
(for emergencies)

AUDIO VISUAL SUPPORT

V : VISTIPS

GOLDEN RULES

Frame
- Use a standard **frame** for all visuals
- Create a **logo** or numbering system

Letters
- Use **LARGE, LEGIBLE LETTERS**
- WORDS ARE NOT VISUALS
- Text 30-50 pts
- Titles 70-100 pts

Images
- Use at least one **IMAGE/LOGO/GRAPH** on every visual

Colour
- Use at least **one colour** more than black on every visual

Kiss
- Keep it short and simple!
- **1** topic. Bullet points and key words
- Six lines maximum
- Six words per line maximum

AUDIO VISUAL SUPPORT

V : THE FLIP CHART

Despite (or maybe because of) the advent of hi-tech, all singing, all dancing PowerPoint software, the good old three-legged faithful friend, the flip chart is **increasing** in popularity with trainers in front of small- to medium-sized audiences.

Why?

- Portable (unlike most projection screens)
- Can be pre-prepared
- Intimate and less formal
- Generative – can be created on the spot, especially with audience input
- FRIENDLY!

V : FLIP TIPS

PREPARATION

INVISIBLE OUTLINE

Lightly pencil in headings in advance when unsure of space, drawing, handwriting etc

CORNER CRIB

Use the top corner to poncil in your notes for each chart. Write small and no one will notice!

READY-MADE

Prepare key charts in advance

AUDIO VISUAL SUPPORT

V : FLIP TIPS

GRAPHICS

ATTRACTIVE
- Give each flip a title
- Use bullet points (like the ones on this page)
- Use at least two dark colours

BIG & BOLD
- Use **thick** markers (bring your own!)
- Should be legible from 10 metres!

CAPITAL KEY WORDS
- Never write sentences!

AUDIO VISUAL SUPPORT

V : FLIP TIPS

GRAPHICS

Whenever possible, use **cartoons** or **drawings** to personalise and add interest to your headings.

AUDIO VISUAL SUPPORT

V : FLIP TIPS

GRAPHICS

Standing

Every time you turn your back on the audience
your voice and their attention disappear.

Since you can't write and face the
audience at the same time (unless
you are a contortionist!)
you should:

- Write (a few words/seconds)
- Turn and talk
- Write (a few words/seconds)
- Turn and talk

V : GRAPHICS

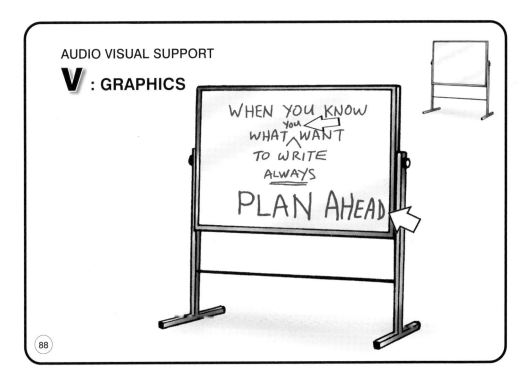

AUDIO VISUAL SUPPORT

V : HEALTH WARNING!

VISUAL VALIUM

Just about every visual aid I've ever seen during a training course
seems to have been designed to send me to sleep – a kind
of visual Valium.

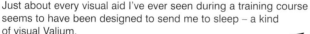

Too many words; too busy; no attempt to use space
properly; no images; little or no colour. After a couple,
I simply can't keep my eyes open.

Unfortunately, with the advent of presentations
software they've become worse! Now they
are professionally bad! Despite what your
corporate identity programme might say,
even a well-designed information
slide becomes sleep-inducing
when the same design
is used over and over
for different messages.

AUDIO VISUAL SUPPORT

V : HEALTH WARNING!

At a recent conference I counted the words and/or numbers on every professional looking slide shown by every particularly unprofessional speaker!

For the 37 slides shown by one earnest presenter, the average per slide was 95 words or figures. The overall conference average was 76 words per slide.

And almost every speaker read almost every one of them! Some of them said, *'You can't read this but what it says is…'* and then proceeded to read them to us. Some just turned to the screen and read them. Some tried but couldn't read them, so we had to try on our own while they talked about something else!

AUDIO VISUAL SUPPORT

V : SLIDE TIPS

Use the 'storyboard' approach:

- One slide with **chapter headings**
- One slide **per** chapter heading
- One slide **per** point/topic in each chapter
- Print series name and number on each
- Concentrate message in centre
- Use only $2/3$ of space for message

NB
USE THE **FLICK** VISTIPS STANDARD! (See page 82)

V : SLIDE TIPS

> Words
> are not visuals, they
> are for listening to!

AUDIO VISUAL SUPPORT

V : SLIDE TIPS

GRAPHIC/CLIP ART

- Example of a slide illustrating that wood burning stoves in Kenya save $25 million a year and help fight deforestation.

V : SLIDE TIPS

GRAPHIC/CLIP ART

- Example of a slide from a financial course, likening the function to a ship's sonar.

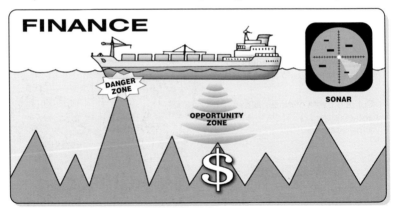

AUDIO VISUAL SUPPORT

V : THE OVERHEAD PROJECTOR

PRODUCING TRANSPARENCIES/SLIDES

Just in case you still have to use an overhead projector, or if Murphy attacks the beamer, or if your CD ROM gets lost:

- Create slides on PowerPoint or similar software (following all the tips)
- Laser print computer-generated visuals directly onto a transparency

Or:

- Cut and paste original artwork and text, then photocopy onto a transparency

Or:

- Write/draw directly onto a transparency (with permanent or non-permanent pens)

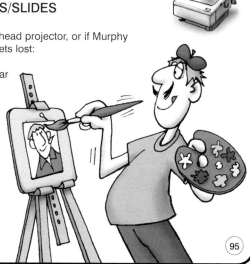

AUDIO VISUAL SUPPORT

V : OVERHEAD PROJECTOR RULES

PROJECTION ANGLE

- How to avoid the 'Keystone' effect:

PROJECTOR
POSITIONING

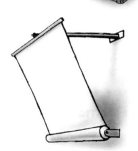

Keep the projector beam at 90° to the screen by tilting the screen (ideal) or by jacking up the projector until keystone disappears; if you jack the projector you'll need a chock to prevent transparencies sliding forward

AUDIO VISUAL SUPPORT

V : O/H TIPS

USING THE PROJECTOR

PREPARE   Prepare transparencies in sleeves; in the right order; unclipped

PLACE   Place a transparency on the projector; align; switch on

POSITION   Do not block any participant's view of the screen; switch off projector between each transparency

AUDIO VISUAL SUPPORT

V : THE WHITEBOARD

WRITING AND STICKING

Write on!
- Replaces blackboard (school memories)
- Great for brainstorming
- Change colour often
- Only use appropriate whiteboard pens

Stick up!
- Use 'Post-it' stickers to create group-work summaries (key phrases only); stick on whiteboard
- Move stickers into columns or categories; use pens to draw bubbles round salient groupings or to make links between stickers

AUDIO VISUAL SUPPORT

V : VIDEO AND DVD

In today's multi-media world, video and DVD are virtually indispensable tools for professional trainers. Here are some advantages and disadvantages of the media:

- Professional, fast-moving
- In tune with participants' background/expectations
- Can be adapted to video projection when monitor not available/too cumbersome

- Few videos give **exactly** the message you want
- Expensive to buy/hire
- Technically subject to Murphy's Law

Tips
Edit your own video clips at home (2 VCR's needed).
Use only snippets which support your message.

V : THE TALKING WALL

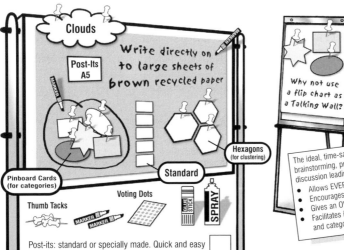

Clouds

Post-Its A5

Write directly on to large sheets of brown recycled paper

Hexagons (for clustering)

Pinboard Cards (for categories)

Standard

Thumb Tacks

Voting Dots

GLUE STICK

SPRAY

Why not use a flip chart as a Talking Wall?

The ideal, time-saving method for brainstorming, problem-solving and discussion leading.
- Allows EVERYONE to participate
- Encourages creative thinking
- Gives an OVERVIEW to all
- Facilitates immediate clustering and categorising

100   Post-its: standard or specially made. Quick and easy

AUDIO VISUAL SUPPORT

H : USING MUSIC AND SOUND EFFECTS

Here are some ways you should be using recorded music in your training course:

- To create a friendly atmosphere at the beginning of the course as participants come in, meet each other and settle down
- As background music during coffee breaks/intervals
- As an introductory 'bang'
- To create specific atmospheres for special messages (film music, theme tunes, sound effects etc)
- To illustrate a point amusingly with a song 'snippet' (example for a course on customer service: 'Help', 'Keep the customer satisfied', 'You can't always get what you want' etc)

AUDIO VISUAL SUPPORT

H : THE CD/MINIDISC/MP3 PLAYER
RECORDED SPEECH

Recorded speech can be useful for:

- Illustrating messages (salesman-customer, boss-subordinate)
- Examples of opinions (market research interviews etc)
- Bringing an absent colleague to the course
- Interjecting humorous anecdotes
- Giving examples of current radio adverts/trends

Use a minidisc to record your session so you can work on your mistakes.

> **Tip** *When recording audio examples, make sure you leave very little space between each recording. In this way you can press the 'pause' button at the end of one example, knowing that the next recording is cued to start as soon as you next hit the button.*

F : ANECDOTES AND METAPHORS

'F' is for Feelings and sensations! 42% of people say that their memories favour this kind of information and, when tested, the same people remember 80% of facts given while 'appealing to feeling' the previous day.

- **ANECDOTES** are true stories which give 'live' examples of what's being presented and help people remember the message. For instance:

    - 'I recall we had one manager who…'
    - 'Someone was working with this software last week and…'

- **METAPHORS** are comparisons/analogies/similes which illustrate what is being presented by comparing it to something very visual or more easily recognisable/understood. They usually start with the phrase, 'It's a bit like…'

    Example: the financial controller's sonar on page 94

F : PARABLES

Parables persuade! They take away the defensive reaction we tend to provoke in participants when we ask them to change the way they do things. Parables (like the 'Prodigal Son') refer to a third party in a 'far away' place and thus feel safe. The participant, nevertheless, connects with the message and projects it onto him/herself which allows SELF-INITIATED change to take place.

AUDIO VISUAL SUPPORT

F : TOUCH, TASTE AND SMELL

TOUCH

Your audience will remember your key points much more clearly if they are INVOLVED. One way to ensure involvement is to give them something to touch. Handouts, samples, models, free gifts – all will help participants to participate and, therefore, remember.

TASTE AND SMELL

On the face of it, it would seem highly inappropriate for you, as a trainer, to ask your participants to taste or smell something! But… think about candy and air fresheners which could simply lend atmosphere to your course and maybe even help link your message to something pleasant in the participants' minds. Even if you don't actually produce smoke in your 'Fire Hazards' course or give them some coffee in your 'HR Services' session, you can always DESCRIBE tastes and smells!

F : CROSS-SENSING

If you'd like to hypnotise your audience, do some 'cross-sensing'! This simply means describing something in a way which appeals to all the senses: SIGHT, HEARING, TOUCH, TASTE, SMELL, HEAT/COLD/PAIN/EMOTIONS.

A manager for a large multinational held her sales audience spellbound for 10 minutes as she described how a magnetic resonance scanner worked by taking them into a hospital in their minds. Some participants reported that they were actually able to feel what it was like to be inside the scanner.

AUDIO VISUAL SUPPORT

MURPHY'S LAW

'If something can go wrong – it will!'

O'Connor's corollary:
'Murphy was an optimist!'

The only way to beat Murphy
is to be a professional and
use the 3 P's:

- **Preparation**
- **Preparation**
- **Preparation**

VIDEO FEEDBACK

Here's an idea to help you accelerate your improvement as a trainer:

Video-tape yourself at one of your next training sessions (remember to ask the audience's permission) and then play the tape back at home.

Give yourself:

- Five objectives to work on for your NEXT course

GROUP & INDIVIDUAL EXERCISES

GROUP & INDIVIDUAL EXERCISES

ICEBREAKERS

Here are **3** ideas for 'inclusion activities' (see pages 49 & 50) to supplement the classic 'please introduce yourself/your neighbour' presentations.

- **2 True, one False**
  Participants introduce themselves by giving one incorrect and two correct pieces of information about their background; likes and dislikes; present job, etc - the group must guess which is true and which false

- **Famous Pairs**
  Write the names of some famous pairs on post-its (Romeo/Juliet, Laurel/Hardy, etc) and stick them at random on participants' backs so they can't see who they are; they must then locate their 'partner' by asking others questions about their identity - these questions may only be answered by Yes or No

- **Stick-up Needs**
  Ask each participant to write 1-3 objectives for attending the course on separate post-its/cards and to stick them on a flip chart or pinboard while explaining to the others; alternatively, you can collect the cards and stick them up - asking for comments as you do so

GROUP & INDIVIDUAL EXERCISES

THE QUIZ

In training courses where facts must be learned it is essential to 'exercise' participants' new knowledge. Written tests are fine but remind people of their school days.

A well-devised quiz will appeal and test at the same time.

Suggestions

- Break group into quiz teams to provoke competition
- Invent different categories of questions (like TV game shows)
- Keep scores on imaginatively designed board (whiteboard/pinwall)
- Don't forget the prizes!

A- TEAM

GROUP & INDIVIDUAL EXERCISES

CASE STUDIES

Case Studies

Concisely written, practical and realistic case studies will induce thinking, analysis, pro and con discussion and genuine efforts to find solutions to problems. Case studies help participants to apply theoretical knowledge to real-life situations and also serve as 'pace-changers' to stimulate interest and attention.

Case Study Rules for Trainers

- Know the facts of case study well
- Have pre-prepared questions to guide trainees during their own analysis of the facts
- Tabulate consensus items during discussion
- Encourage differences of opinion to explore alternative solutions
- The trainer should use Socratic Direction (see page 64) to summarise learning points from the case study

GROUP & INDIVIDUAL EXERCISES

VIDEO RECORDING

Nowadays video cameras are idiot and almost Murphy-proof! Recording trainees in individual or group practice sessions is a very powerful teaching tool!

TIPS

- Use a digital camcorder for easy access to recorded tracks
- Prepare connections to the TV monitor in advance to avoid delay
- Use fast forward during playback to save time
- If you have the equipment, record separate individuals/groups on different tapes/CDs and split into sub groups for playback

People are hyper-sensitive about seeing themselves on video
First reactions of trainees who are not used to the medium concern their **hairstyle**, their **weight** and their **accent**
Even when they accept their **look** and **sound** they may over-react with self-criticism and become depressed or defensive

 Always accept these reactions with sympathy and sensitivity, and stress confidentiality. Use professional feedback technique (see page 115)

ROLE-PLAYING 1

Role-playing

Role-playing is a dramatised form of case study in which trainees act out a human relations problem under the guidance of the trainer who elicits an evaluation of the performance in light of previously taught principles.

Pre-requisites for a successful role-playing exercise:

- The role play situation must be realistic
- The situation must be one with which participants can identify; characters should be of a type that really exists in the organisation
- Participants must live their parts
- Role-playing should not represent a threat to timid participants
- Trainer should play the 'challenger' role

Role-playing is not play acting. It is 'reality practice'.

GROUP & INDIVIDUAL EXERCISES

ROLE-PLAYING FEEDBACK RULES

1. First ask role-player(s) for an 'auto-critique'
2. Ask group to take notes and watch the video re-play (where appropriate)
3. Ask the group to give feedback

Rules

- Always separate 'motivational' from 'developmental' feedback
- For developmental feedback, use the conditional tense and always offer an alternative (ie: 'I think it would have been more effective if you had ...')
- Always address the individual concerned and say 'you' not 'he/she'

GROUP & INDIVIDUAL EXERCISES

PROJECT WORK

Projects

In modular courses and seminars, given at regular intervals, (weekly, monthly, etc) project work between sessions provides an ideal bridging, learning and review experience.

1. **Tailor-made**   As a trainer you should develop relevant project structures which will allow trainees to practise each session's learning points - if possible in groups of 4-7

2. **Canned**   Many video-based packages exist which provide inter-session project work as an integral part of the course

GROUP & INDIVIDUAL EXERCISES

PROJECT WORK

THE GROUP RECAP

One kind of project worth highlighting is the group recap.

In courses which last more than one day, split the group into small teams and ask a different team to make a resumé of the previous day's learning at the start of each new day.

Teams invariably vie with one another to make **their** resumé the best (at least the most amusing), a lot of learning takes place and a good time is had by all (especially the trainer who has one less module to present!).

GROUP & INDIVIDUAL EXERCISES

INSTRUMENTS

Seminar Instruments

3 examples of instruments which can be used to develop or sustain interest, provide a point, gather information, etc.

● Matrix	● Grid/Window	● Questionnaire

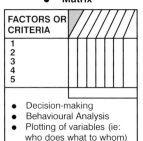

- Decision-making
- Behavioural Analysis
- Plotting of variables (ie: who does what to whom)

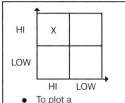

- To plot a combination of 2 characteristics

```
1 _____
2 _____
3 _____
4 _____
5 _____
6 _____
7 _____
```

- Self-awareness
- Attitude survey
- Polling facts

FURTHER READING AND VIEWING

Learning

'Preparing Instructional Objectives' by Robert Mager, Kogan Page

'Superlearning' by Ostrander & Schroeder, Sphere

'The Adult Learner - a neglected species' by Malcolm Knowles, Gulf

'Learning to Listen, Learning to Teach' by Jane Vella, Jossey-Bass

'Accelerated Learning' and *'Music to Learn By'* from author Roger Swartz, Essential
  Medical Information Systems, Box 1607, Durant, OK 74702-1607, USA

'The Learner's Pocketbook' by Paul Hayden, Management Pocketbooks

General

'Techniques of Training' by Leslie Rae, Gower

'Training Costs Analysis' by Glenn E Heard, ASTD

'Improving Trainer Effectiveness' edited by Roger Bennett, Gower

'Instructor Excellence' by Bob Powers, Jossey-Bass

'Active Training' by Mel Silberman, Lexington

'The In-House Trainer as Consultant' by Holdaway & Saunders, Kogan Page

FURTHER READING AND VIEWING

General (continued)

'Successful Training Practice' by Alan Anderson, Blackwell

'A Handbook for Training Strategy' by Martyn Sloman, Gower

'Facilitating' by Mike Robson, Gower

'Influencing with Integrity (NLP)' by Genie Laborde, Syntony

'Graphics for Presenters' from author Lynn Kearney at 5379 Broadway, Oakland, CA
  94618, USA

Video: *'Ten Training Tips'*, John Townsend, Melrose Film Productions

Brains and Memory

'Your Memory - a User's Guide' by Allan Baddeley, Pelican

'Make the Most of your Mind' by Tony Buzan, Pan

'Mind Mapping and Memory' by Ingemar Svantesson, Kogan Page

'Mind and Brain' from Scientific American,

Mindpower (video tapes) by Tony Buzan, BBC

'Brain Mind', monthly, edited by Marilyn Ferguson, Box 42211, Los Angeles, CA 90042, USA

Video: *'Memories are Made of this'*, John Townsend, Melrose Film Productions

THE MANAGEMENT POCKETBOOK SERIES

Pocketbooks

Appraisals
Assertiveness
Balance Sheet
Business Planning
Business Writing
Call Centre Customer Care
Career Transition
Challengers
Coaching
Communicator's
Competencies
Controlling Absenteeism
Creative Manager's
C.R.M.
Cross-cultural Business
Cultural Gaffes
Customer Service
Decision-making
Developing People
Discipline
Diversity
E-commerce
Emotional Intelligence
Employment Law
Empowerment

Energy and Well-being
Facilitator's
Flexible Workplace
Handling Complaints
Icebreakers
Impact & Presence
Improving Efficiency
Improving Profitability
Induction
Influencing
International Trade
Interviewer's
I.T. Trainer's
Key Account Manager's
Leadership
Learner's
Manager's
Managing Budgets
Managing Cashflow
Managing Change
Managing Recruitment
Managing Upwards
Managing Your Appraisal
Marketing
Meetings

Mentoring
Motivation
Negotiator's
Networking
NLP
Openers & Closers
People Manager's
Performance Management
Personal Success
Positive Mental Attitude
Presentations
Problem Behaviour
Problem Solving
Project Management
Quality
Resolving Conflict
Sales Excellence
Salesperson's
Self-managed Development
Starting In Management
Strategy
Stress
Succeeding at Interviews
Teambuilding Activities
Teamworking

Telephone Skills
Telesales
Thinker's
Time Management
Trainer Standards
Trainer's
Training Evaluation
Training Needs Analysis
Virtual Teams
Vocal Skills

Pocketsquares

Great Training Robbery
Hook Your Audience

Pocketfiles

Trainer's Blue Pocketfile of
Ready-to-use Activities

Trainer's Green Pocketfile of
Ready-to-use Activities

Trainer's Red Pocketfile of
Ready-to-use Activities

27.2.06

About the Author

John Townsend, BA MA MCIPD

John has built a reputation internationally as a leading trainer of trainers. He is the founder of the highly-regarded Master Trainer Institute, a total learning facility located just outside Geneva which draws trainers and facilitators from around the world. He set up the Institute after 30 years' experience in international consulting and human resource management positions in the UK, France, the United States and Switzerland.

From 1978–1984 he was European Director of Executive Development with GTE in Geneva with training responsibility for over 800 managers in some 15 countries. John has published a number of management and professional guides and regularly contributes articles to leading management and training journals.

In addition to training trainers, he is also a regular speaker at conferences and leadership seminars throughout Europe.

Contact:
John Townsend, The Master Trainer Institute,
L'Avant Centre, 13 chemin du Levant, Ferney-Voltaire, France
Tel: (33) 450 42 84 16   Fax: (33) 450 40 57 37
www.mt-institute.com

ORDER FORM

Your details

Name _____

Position _____

Company _____

Address _____

_____

_____

Telephone _____

Fax _____

E-mail _____

VAT No. (EC companies) _____

Your Order Ref _____

Please send me:

	No. copies
The Trainer's _____ Pocketbook	☐
The _____ Pocketbook	☐
The _____ Pocketbook	☐
The _____ Pocketbook	☐
The _____ Pocketbook	☐

Order by Post

MANAGEMENT POCKETBOOKS LTD

LAUREL HOUSE, STATION APPROACH,
ALRESFORD, HAMPSHIRE SO24 9JH UK

Order by Phone, Fax or Internet

Telephone: +44 (0)1962 735573
Facsimile: +44 (0)1962 733637
E-mail: sales@pocketbook.co.uk
Web: www.pocketbook.co.uk

MANAGEMENT POCKETBOOKS